MW00679267

*For Your Birthday,
I Wish . . .*

For Your Birthday, I Wish . . .

350 Wishes for the
Happiest of Birthdays

Written and illustrated by
Lorraine Bodger

**Andrews McMeel
Publishing**

Kansas City

00 01 02 03 04 TWP 10 9 8 7 6 5 4 3 2 1

ISBN: 0-7407-0991-7

Library of Congress Catalog Card Number: 00-101320

Book design by Lisa Martin

Introduction

When you receive this book from a friend, you'll know you've been singled out for exceptional birthday attention: 350 wishes to delight you, inspire you, and make you laugh. Your friend is acknowledging your special day and wishing you the very best. She wants you to enjoy it to the max!

Your birthday is meant to be that particular occasion—yours alone—when your loved ones are thinking of you, doing things for you, honoring your very existence. This can be delicious and thrilling, but sometimes a little daunting, so *For Your Birthday, I Wish . . .* is here to help you add your current birthday to your stock of great memories.

This is where you'll find dozens of wishes for birthday celebrations of all kinds, practical and outrageous, realistic and fantastic. There are birthday ideas to think about, birthday activities to do, birthday gifts to ask for and to give yourself, words of encouragement, and plenty of reminders about how good life is. And since birthdays come only once each year, you'll find dozens of just plain terrific wishes for every other day, too.

When you read this little book, you'll look at birthdays in a completely positive way: A birthday is a perfect moment to make exciting plans and devise wonderful things to look forward to. It's an opportunity for evaluation and strategy: Think about the quality of your life over this past year (did you have enough fun? did you work too hard?) and what you want for the coming year (is it time for a trip—or a new boyfriend?). Think about the ways in which you want to change (are you ready for a new hairstyle or a new job?), and ways you don't want to change (keep that waistline trim!).

Birthdays are occasions for every kind of pleasure and pampering, and your birthday is all yours to celebrate however you like. You're a whole year smarter and wiser and prettier, you know better who you are and where you're going, you have experience and an interesting history and lots more confidence.

So please accept these 350 wishes for a very happy birthday (and every day)—this year, next year, and for years to come.

For Your Birthday, I Wish That . . .

Your best friend lets you know there's going to be a
surprise party for you, so you don't get caught in
your pajamas with curlers in your hair.

◎

You have breakfast on the terrace . . . in Tuscany.

◎

Every birthday present you receive
is something you want.

◎

You wake up on your birthday morning and
discover you've lost three pounds.

You do something really wild:
Take flying lessons. Trek the Himalayas. Build a
treehouse. Learn to belly dance. Write a novel.

◎

The trainer at the gym tells you
how great your abs are looking.

◎

Your coworkers take you out
for a fabulous birthday lunch.

◎

Your sweetheart takes you out
for a candlelit birthday dinner.

◎

You have the birthday party of your dreams.

◎

You open an oyster and find a pearl.

You get twice as many
birthday cards as
you were expecting.

It suddenly hits you: Many of the things
that were hard for you to do a few years ago
are easy now. So what does that say about
the things that are hard for you now?

The wish you make when you
blow out all the candles with
one breath comes true!

Your favorite TV program is
renewed for another season.

You get to leave for your vacation on your birthday.

You make your first million before you're forty.
And your second before you're fifty.

Your next business trip takes you
to a place you actually want to go.

◎

The baby-sitter stays for the entire afternoon so you
can go out and indulge yourself—shopping, a
museum, a bike ride, whatever you love to do.

◎

Your cat allergy magically disappears
so you can adopt that adorable
kitten you've always wanted.

◎

You play back your messages, and every
one of them is a birthday greeting.

◎

This is the year you finally start to feel mature.

You have abundant energy to
carry out your most ambitious plans.

◎

There are no bills in the mail on your
birthday, and no junk, either.

◎

Someone takes you out to lunch for no
reason but the pleasure of your company.

◎

Your favorite restaurant hears
it's your birthday and sends you
a fancy dessert with a candle.
And the waitstaff sings "Happy Birthday."

◎

You never have a fashion emergency.

There's plenty of time today to swing in
a hammock or lie on a beach or take a long walk
in the woods to renew and refresh yourself.

You meet a celebrity and find
out that he's . . . not too bright.

You grow into your looks and become
more beautiful as you get older.

Today it's strictly forbidden to do
anything you don't feel like doing. Including
getting dressed. Or brushing your teeth.
Or making the bed. Get the idea?

Your next haircut is your best haircut.

The florist delivers
a giant birthday bouquet
from a secret admirer.

The coming year sees your most
cherished wishes granted. And you're
careful what you wish for.

◎

Your children are healthy and happy,
and grow up to be your friends.

◎

There's as much pleasure in
looking toward the future as there
is in looking back at the past.

◎

The bank makes a mistake in your favor.

◎

Someone brings you a birthday
breakfast in bed, with a rose on the tray.

You're never embarrassed by:
spinach in your teeth
a huge run in your panty hose
a smudge on your nose
a rip in the seat of your pants.

◎

You never hear the words "I told you so."

◎

You're blessed with friends who listen
carefully to you and guard your secrets like
their own, friends who take time for you,
care for you, stick by you, rejoice with you.

◎

There's quiet time for you to enjoy,
before everyone else wakes up or after
everyone else has gone to sleep.

You never have to stand in line at the movies.

◎

You receive that good thing that
comes in a small package: a diamond ring,
a check for your college tuition, an airline ticket,
a luscious chocolate brownie.

◎

Beloved Fido (or Muffy or Baxter or
Squeaky or Daisy) lives to a ripe old age.

◎

You toss your diet to the winds, but just for today.

◎

There's a pot of fresh coffee ready
and waiting when you stagger into
the kitchen each morning.

You forgive yourself for the mistakes
you've made and love yourself for
all the things you've done right.

One of your birthday presents is a
gift certificate to your favorite store.

The fortunes in your fortune
cookies are always rosy.

You spend an evening waltzing in the
world's most romantic dress, with the
world's most romantic man.

Your special day starts out
great and just gets better.

You give yourself a bouquet of seasonal
flowers once a month for a year.

◉

Someone you love gives you a kiss for
every year, and one more to grow on.

◉

You have no regrets.

◉

Your good-luck charm brings you the very best luck.

◉

You regress to adolescence and throw
a birthday slumber party for your closest
girlfriends. Stay up giggling all night, and hey!
your mother will not come in and tell you to
settle down. Don't forget the pillow fight.

This year you try out for that
job you've always wanted and didn't
have the nerve to apply for.

◎

You make a list of ten things you accomplished
during the past twelve months. Give yourself a big
pat on the back for each one, and a nice reward, too.

◎

You make a list of ten things you'd
like to do before your next birthday, from
the sublime to the ridiculous. Check off the
items as you accomplish them.

◎

You rest all day and birthday-party all night.

◎

You learn to tango.

You spread happiness: Make a match
between two friends you think will
be ideal for each other.

◉

Just when you're least expecting it,
you fall head over heels in love.

◉

You take the time to do whatever makes
you feel really good. And you do it often.

◉

Your sweetheart gives you a gift you
don't even know you want until you open
the package and shriek for joy!

◉

An artist stops you in the street
and begs you to sit for him.

The birthday cake is so
delicious that it's all gone
by the end of the party.

You think the delicious cake is
all gone, and then you find that your
best friend has wrapped up a big piece
of it and stashed it in the fridge for you.

◎

You break your bad habits for good.

◎

This year you live in the here and now,
and let tomorrow wait its turn.

◎

A personal assistant is yours
for a whole month.

◎

Your big birthday present is
a week at a health resort.

In order to save your energy for
the activities you really love, you choose the
easy way: a suitcase with rollers, nonstick pans,
self-cleaning oven, take-out dinners.

You stop trying to please everyone else
and start trying to please yourself.

Today the kids clean their
rooms without being asked.

You bake a batch of birthday cookies,
all for yourself. Eat them warm from the
oven with a glass of cold milk.

Your ship comes in.

Your sweetheart takes you to the Tunnel
of Love and makes your toes curl.

◎

You buy yourself a pair of really cool sunglasses.
(And stop that wrinkle-making squinting!)

◎

In a moment of utter brilliance,
you figure out a filing system that
works perfectly for you.

◎

You do something spontaneous on
your birthday and surprise yourself!

◎

Suddenly you realize you look fabulous
without makeup . . . or with it.

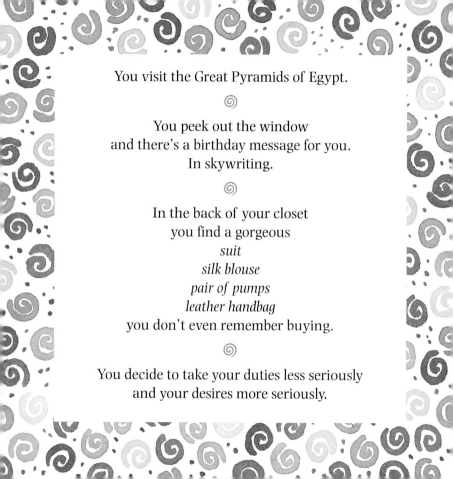

You visit the Great Pyramids of Egypt.

You peek out the window
and there's a birthday message for you.
In skywriting.

In the back of your closet
you find a gorgeous
suit
silk blouse
pair of pumps
leather handbag
you don't even remember buying.

You decide to take your duties less seriously
and your desires more seriously.

You're having such a good
time that you forget to eat.

＊

The car starts immediately on cold mornings.

＊

Your voice mailbox is
loaded with birthday greetings.

＊

Not a moment too soon, you parlay
that great gizmo, gadget, game, recipe,
or concept into the profitable business
career you were meant to have.

＊

You kick back, relax, and let someone
else run the show for you on your birthday.

The sun shines for you.

You come to regard the signs
of aging as signs of achievement.

◎

You realize that you enjoy your own company.

◎

It's a good day for a change of style: If you usually
wear suits, put on something loose and flowing. If
you usually wear sweats, dress up in something
sleek and tailored. How do you feel?

◎

You hit the roof, throw a tantrum, punch a pillow,
scream at the top of your lungs, go bananas—and
get it out of your system, for heaven's sake.

◎

Your darling brings you an
old-fashioned gardenia corsage.

Your big jar of pennies is finally full, and it adds up
to dinner for two at your favorite bistro.

◎

You get happily tipsy with
your girlfriends on your birthday.

◎

From now on you earn your
living doing something you love.

◎

You place an ad in the personals and
someone truly wonderful turns up.

◎

The strategy meeting is going around in circles,
and you raise the point that brings
it to a stunned and admiring halt.

You spend less time
on the phone
on the road
on the Internet
in front of the TV
in the kitchen.

You spend more time
with your kids
with your friends
reading books
at the movies
in bed.

You tear up that "Happy Birthday"
greeting from the AARP.

Someone makes you a dozen
birthday cupcakes with buttercream
frosting and chocolate sprinkles.

◎

You hit the ball out of the park. Twice.

◎

You yield to temptation.

◎

You come home from work on your birthday and
find that all your chores have been done.

◎

You treat yourself to beautiful
stationery and business cards.

◎

You acquire a gorgeous new wardrobe.

A dear friend makes a tape of your favorite pieces of
music to play at your birthday party.

◎

You have thrills and chills when you're in the mood
and peace and quiet when you're not.

◎

Starting today you see yourself as the people who
love you do: smart, funny, kind, compassionate,
helpful, generous, interesting, hardworking.

◎

This year you have the pleasure of enlarging
your kitchen
your garden
your income
your circle of friends
your mind.

You realize the benefits of getting older:
Minor mistakes don't turn you into a basket case.
The things that used to embarrass you, don't.
You're a whole lot less dependent than you once
were. You have your own opinions. Way to go.

Your lover gives you a sexy,
satin-and-lace, peekaboo nightgown.

You do something crazy and fun that makes your
kids groan and say "Oh, M-o-o-o-o-m!"

You treat yourself to home delivery of the morning
paper, weekdays and weekends.

You see your friends more often.

You stop postponing your
a) dreams
b) ambitions
c) goals
d) promises
e) all of the above

You float over your troubles in a
balloon, a glider, or even a swing.

If your birthday is in summer:
Have a bash at the beach or lake.
Barbecue a birthday dinner.
Fill a basket with zinnias, dahlias, snapdragons.
Take a vacation.
Catch fireflies.

If your birthday is in autumn:
Drive a country road to see the changing leaves.
Drop in at a farm stand for apples, pears, pumpkins,
and maple syrup. Line your front porch with pots
of chrysanthemums. Enjoy the nippy air.

If your birthday is in winter:
Host a fancy holiday party, so you can
dazzle your guests with your prettiest outfit.
Decorate the house with bright red amaryllis.
Go sledding at dusk. Make hot cocoa.

If your birthday is in spring:
Trim an Easter bonnet.
Eat lots of asparagus and strawberries.
Buy a big bouquet of lilacs and daffodils.
Walk in the rain. Make a fresh start.

This year you make it to the
finish line in the marathon race.

◎

You hit the Big Apple for
a week of Broadway shows.

◎

You have the love life you've
always dreamed of.

◎

You're Queen for a Day.

◎

Your sweetheart becomes your fiancé.

◎

You eat as many potato chips as you want.

This year you graduate
from junk food to real food.

Guess what? You don't need
anyone else's permission to:
stay out late
go to an R-rated movie
play video games for hours
have another ice-cream cone
paint your toenails green.

◎

You drop your extremely smart suggestions
into the office suggestion box—and your
boss decides to put them all into effect.

◎

You take a birthday moment or two
for thinking about where you are right now
and where you want to go in the future.

◎

You have dinner at a four-star restaurant.

Everyone in your life appreciates
you—and tells you how much!

You visit the children's section of your local
bookstore. Sit on one of those tiny chairs and read
all the books you loved when you were a kid.

Today you and a friend go to a playground
and do it all: the seesaw, the swings, the slide,
the monkey bars. Who cares if the little kids
think you're over the age limit?

You buy a bottle of very good wine
and sip it slowly to savor the difference
between it and your everyday bottle.

You have flair.

Purely for the fun of it,
you sign up for a total makeover.

◎

You take a vacation at
a) a ranch in the mountains
b) a cabin in the woods
c) a cottage at the shore
d) a penthouse in the city
e) all of the above

◎

You're invited to be a guest on *Oprah*.

◎

You go to the movies every night for a week.

◎

Your mother (or father or grandmother) sends you
recipes for all the foods you loved in childhood.

Today you let other people do things for you:
get you a cup of coffee, put the grocery bags in
the car, pick up the laundry, load the dishwasher,
return the library book, make you a martini.

⊚

You curl up on the couch with hot buttered popcorn
and a videotape of that terrific film you missed.

⊚

Today you set aside half an hour to snuggle with
your sweetie before the business of the day begins.

⊚

The emcee invites you up to the mike to belt out
a song, and you knock the audience dead.

⊚

Under your tailored suit you're wearing your real
self— slinky silk, trimmed with ribbons and lace.

A good friend gives you a microcassette
recorder for your birthday, so you can get
your thoughts, reminders, and notes down
on tape before you forget them.

◎

Congratulations! You've just won
a lifetime supply of pistachio nuts.

◎

With the miracle of computers and e-mail, you
complete the day's work in your pajamas. By noon.

◎

You figure out what a perfect birthday
would be, and then you go get it.

◎

Your kids tell you you're cool.

You and your longtime buddies sit around
playing "Remember when . . ." until you're
laughing so hard you fall on the floor.

◎

You acknowledge and congratulate
yourself on your own competence.

◎

You give your car a birthday present:
new rubber mats, rack to hold your favorite CDs,
backrest, over-the-seat organizer, tool kit.

◎

Some thoughtful, generous soul stocks
your freezer with gourmet meals and an extra
quart of your favorite ice cream.

◎

The folks at *People* magazine call you for an interview.

One of your high school boyfriends
phones you unexpectedly, you rendezvous
at a romantic bar, and next thing you know,
the two of you are an item.

◎

Your hometown wants to
name a park in your honor.

◎

You start a birthday tradition:
Take your mother out for dinner. Buy a new hat.
Go to the theater. Your birthday, your choice.

◎

Acting age-appropriate is fine 90 percent
of the time. The other 10 percent, go wild!

◎

You do something completely silly, just for the fun of it.

*Your whole gang meets at
a Chinese restaurant for
a big birthday feast for you.*

No one tells you how you should feel, today
or any other day. And if they do tell you, ignore
them. You're entitled to your own feelings.

꩜

You do something utterly unlike
yourself, just for an experiment.

꩜

Today you make time to enjoy
a special breakfast instead of grabbing
a yogurt as you dash out of the house.

꩜

You receive a pair of tickets to that special concert,
game, or show you've been wanting to see.

꩜

You're invited to a private screening
of the next blockbuster movie.

You go home expecting to find an empty
refrigerator and discover instead that it's
chock-full of your favorite foods.

◎

You set a goal for your next
birthday and start on it today.

◎

When you're clearing the junk out of
the attic, you find an authentic Warhol.

◎

You build yourself a (large or small)
wine cellar and stock it with goodies.

◎

Today the right someone devotes
a few hours to kissing you—and
kissing you and kissing you.

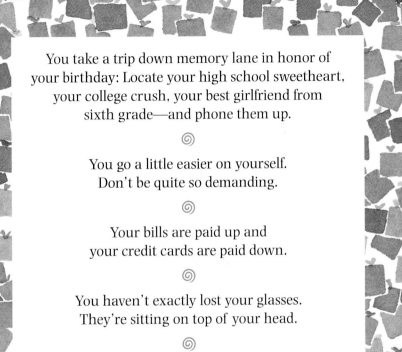

You take a trip down memory lane in honor of
your birthday: Locate your high school sweetheart,
your college crush, your best girlfriend from
sixth grade—and phone them up.

You go a little easier on yourself.
Don't be quite so demanding.

Your bills are paid up and
your credit cards are paid down.

You haven't exactly lost your glasses.
They're sitting on top of your head.

You remember everyone's name.

One of your friends hires a pianist
for your birthday party, and you all sing songs
around the piano for hours on end.

◎

Another friend hires a fortune teller
for your party, and she gazes into her crystal
ball to see wonderful futures for everyone.

◎

A third friend hires a caricature artist for the party,
and she makes a hilarious portrait of each guest.

◎

You dine your way across
Italy
France
Japan
New York City.

There's a display of
fireworks especially for
your birthday.

You give yourself permission to
bask in the sun
lounge on a deck
loll on a beach
lie in a field
stretch out in a lawn chair
and relax.

◎

You get yourself a cordless headset
phone and give your neck a rest.

◎

This year you decide not only
to register to vote, but to vote, too.

◎

One of your friends takes lots
of pictures at your birthday party,
so you'll have the memories forever.

You have the good sense to stop overworking,
whether you're doing too much paperwork
or housework or volunteer work.

✺

You kick up your heels: Learn to do a somersault,
a cartwheel, and a headstand!

✺

You buy yourself a set of towels
so soft that they make you feel as if
you're being stroked by gentle hands.

✺

You buy yourself a set of sheets that make you feel
as if you're lying in a garden full of flowers.

✺

A kind aunt tackles your basket of mending:
hems put up, buttons sewn on, seams stitched.

You have a shopping
spree in a candy store.

You act the age you feel,
even if it isn't the age you are.

֍

You find a birthday poem
slipped under your door.

֍

This year you smooth out the rough spots
in your most important relationship.

֍

You find a $20 bill in the pocket of your jeans.

֍

You pass physics.

֍

Some joker gives you a gold lamé
shower cap for your birthday.

This year the holidays fulfill
all your expectations.

◎

Your hair never turns gray, but if it
does, you either love it or you have absolutely
no ambivalence about coloring it.

◎

This year you declare your independence from
something you can really do without: a fear of
flying, a bad boyfriend, a rotten job, a closet
full of clothes you haven't worn in years.

◎

You reverse the usual order of aging:
Instead of letting your brain capacity decrease
and your hip measurement increase . . .
see where we're going with this?

Starting today you get enough exercise.

◎

Starting today you get enough rest.

◎

Starting today you make the
first move toward organizing your
a) finances
b) desk
c) relationships
d) bureau drawers
e) all of the above

◎

You have a revelation.

◎

When you go to the library, the very book you're
dying to read jumps off the shelf into your hands.

At least once a week you have plenty of laughs.

◎

Among the ordinary, you find a little extraordinary.

◎

Your sweetie takes you to a glamorous
cabaret for your birthday to drink champagne
cocktails and listen to a chanteuse doing
a medley of romantic tunes.

◎

Your sweetie takes you to a hot jazz
club for your birthday, and the riffs are so
awesome that you stay until the wee hours.

◎

You buy Moroccan rugs in Morocco,
Venetian glass in Venice, Belgian lace
in Belgium, and Irish linen in Ireland.

When you want a snack,
the very snack you crave
is waiting for you.

You assume the serious role your age
bestows upon you, and have a food fight at dinner.

◎

If you've been resisting computer
literacy, you buy a computer and learn to use it.
If they can do it, you can do it.

◎

The ice-cream man stops right at your corner.

◎

You have smooth sailing.

◎

You catch on that the older you get, the less
desirable it is to be as scrawny as a model.

◎

You acknowledge that the older you get,
the less desirable it is to be fat.

This year you free yourself from the tyranny of
houseplants
fashion
e-mail
the telephone.

◎

You flip on your favorite radio station and hear a
song dedicated to you for your birthday.

◎

You give your house a birthday present—a fresh
coat of paint, new windows, clean gutters,
rosebushes—to make it spiffy for the new year.

◎

You're not afraid to ask for help when you need it.

◎

You never flub the punch lines of the jokes you tell.

You find the perfect designer dress on the
clearance rack, in your size, at 60 percent off.

◎

Instead of having one big party,
you spread your birthday celebrations over
a week (or even two weeks!): lunches, dinners,
and parties with friends, lovers, and family.

◎

Today someone washes your car,
vacuums the interior, and disposes of all those
empty juice cans and crumpled tissues.

◎

You have dry feet in the rain
and warm feet in the snow.

◎

A friend makes you a Happy Birthday bumper sticker.

Someone gives you a membership to a
great gym (with a pool!) for your birthday.

◎

This year you make a date with
the guy you've admired from afar
and haven't had the courage to call.

◎

Your mother sends you that boxful of
your old toys, drawings, trophies, and high
school mementos she's been keeping for you.

◎

Once a week you get to play
tennis
music
bridge
footsie.

This year you learn to stop eating
when you've had enough food.

◎

You have the feeling of gratification
that comes with doing something for others:
volunteering, making a donation, tutoring,
collecting for a good cause.

◎

You savor a day without time: no watch,
no clock, no calendar, no date book.

◎

You buy yourself a birthday present
you never dreamed you'd buy: a ten-speed bike,
a black lace bra, a ticket to Madrid,
an oil painting, a cell phone, a puppy.

You take a trip to
a toy store to buy
anything you want.

Someone gives you a present you'd never give yourself: a complete ski outfit (including skis), emeralds, a short-wave radio, an espresso maker, a lemon tree, a silver Rolls Royce.

◎

You start looking your age (if you're always carded) or you stop looking your age (if salespeople are always calling you "ma'am").

◎

This year you learn to cut out all the unimportant stuff so you'll have lots of time for the important stuff.

◎

To thank your dad for everything he's done for you, you take him out for an afternoon of whatever entertainment he enjoys most.

You have a friend who adores your sense
of humor, and a friend who knows your dark
side and loves you anyway; an older friend who
gives you good advice, and a younger one who
keeps you up to date; a friend from childhood,
and a brand-new friend; a friend who's like a
good sister, and another who's like a good mother;
a friend at work, and a friend at home.

You throw a birthday party
with a treasure hunt.

This year you decide what you
want to be when you grow up.

This year you dare to be different.

The ginkgo biloba really helps your memory.

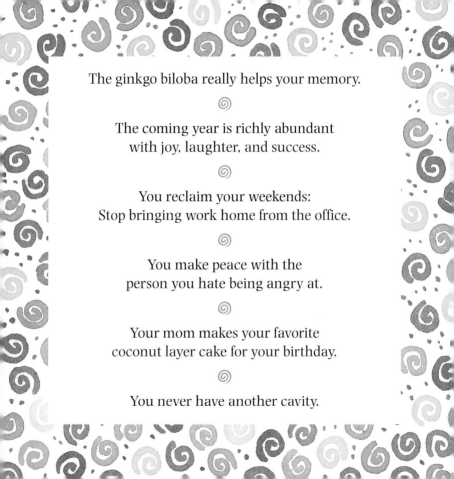

The coming year is richly abundant
with joy, laughter, and success.

You reclaim your weekends:
Stop bringing work home from the office.

You make peace with the
person you hate being angry at.

Your mom makes your favorite
coconut layer cake for your birthday.

You never have another cavity.

You realize you're not obliged
to lie about your age anymore.

❂

You and your lover have a
midday tryst at a chic hotel.

❂

You do or wear whatever makes you feel saucy.

❂

Today you have time to linger over
your morning tea or coffee in bed, on the
sunporch, or under a shady tree.

❂

This year you move away from home.

❂

This year your kids move away from home.

*The baby sleeps
through the night.*

You treat yourself to a long, luxurious
bath instead of your usual speedy shower.

◎

You boldly go where no one has ever gone before.

◎

You pull out all the stops.

◎

You start off the birthday morning with
something delicious, warm from the oven.

◎

You're the guest of honor at a dinner
to celebrate your accomplishments.

◎

Your problems disappear as
quickly as rain puddles in sunshine.

Someone wonderful kidnaps you and whisks you away to an island paradise for a birthday weekend.

◎

This year you overcome your fear of failure—and your fear of success.

◎

You spend a whole day rewarding yourself with things you love to do: movies, shopping, listening to music, kayaking, reading, anything at all. Have a delicious lunch (perhaps a picnic?) and a quiet dinner with a glass (or two?) of wine.

◎

You stumble upon the world's greatest tag sale.

◎

The light of your life wakes you early this morning to say happy birthday by making sweet love to you.

You paint your
ceiling sky blue.

You take time to get started on a project you've been
thinking about and just haven't had a moment for.

This year you finish your education—high school,
technical school, college, or grad school.

Head-to-toe pampering is the order
of the day: shampoo and conditioning,
toning mask, massage, pedicure.

You have something made especially for you: face
powder, a pair of earrings, leather sandals, a
handsome desk, shelves for your shoes, a blend of
tea, monogrammed towels, a bathing suit.

Your goals are firm and your path is clear.

You have exactly the right
outfit for every occasion.

◎

Today you start your retirement
account without moaning and
groaning about getting old.

◎

There are love notes and chocolate hearts hidden all
over the house—where you'll find them.

◎

Your true love reads aloud to you, preferably in bed.

◎

Your true love sings you a lullaby.

◎

Your true love tucks you in and kisses you good night.

Your favorite
stuffed animal
coffee mug
backpack
bedroom slippers
last forever.

⊚

Your horoscope in today's
paper is a real winner.

⊚

When you go to have your hair done
today (for your birthday) there's a brand-new
issue of your favorite magazine.

⊚

A multiplex theater opens within
walking distance of your home, so you can
go to the movies at the drop of a hat.

You have your cake and eat it, too:
Buy one big cake for your birthday party and
another small one for you to enjoy tomorrow.

◎

When you work overtime, you get paid overtime.

◎

Your kids never lay a guilt trip on you.

◎

Your best friend tells your mate about the
present you said you wanted more than anything
in the world, and he gets it for you.

◎

Your Uncle Dexter sends you a generous
birthday check to spend any way you please.

◎

You believe in yourself.

You fly the
Concorde to Paris.

bon anniversaire

If you happen to receive a birthday windfall,
you share some of it with your partner.

◎

A secret pal cleans your oven, defrosts
your refrigerator, and scrubs your bathroom.

◎

You wise up and stop worrying about what your
a) parents
b) mother-in-law
c) older sister
d) boyfriend
e) all of the above
think of what you do.

◎

A good friend makes a contribution
to your favorite charity in your name.

Today you cancel your appointments,
forget about your obligations, and throw
caution to the winds. It's your birthday!

◎

You give yourself a state-of-the-art sound system.

◎

You search out a terrific moisturizer
and start using it. Every day.

◎

This year you reconnect with a person
you haven't seen in a very long time—someone
you'd like to have back in your life.

◎

You do something new and exciting
on the first day of every month for a year.

You decide to buy a chaise longue
for your bedroom.

◎

You decide to buy yourself a supersoft
cashmere-blend throw for snuggling up
on the new chaise on chilly nights.

◎

You have the satisfying experience of
being part of a smoothly performing team
at work, at school, or at play.

◎

What you want is what you need, and vice versa.

◎

Your best friend takes you out for a birthday
high tea, with finger sandwiches, miniature tarts,
and lots of itty-bitty cookies.

Someone brings you a bottle of extremely good champagne (and maybe a little caviar to go with it?).

⊚

You throw a birthday party with kid stuff: pin the tail on the donkey, balloons, favors, funny hats, and a magician.

⊚

You take a cruise and have a shipboard romance.

⊚

You always remember the sunscreen.

⊚

Yours is the winning bid at the auction.

⊚

You and your partner find time to play together.

The movie you love best in all the world is on TV today.

◎

All your blind dates turn out to be winners.

◎

The people you work with are
inventive, inspiring, intriguing, industrious,
informed, insightful. And nice, too.

◎

Today you decide to skip all your boring chores.

◎

Your best pal writes a special
birthday song about you.

◎

You spin the globe, put your finger down—
and take a trip to wherever it touches.

You learn to snorkel.

Today you have time to listen
to your favorite CDs.

This year you
install a hot tub
build storage in the garage
make a garden
remodel the kitchen
add another bathroom
to improve your home life.

Someone gives you a library of
Books on Tape for your birthday.

You treat yourself to a refreshing
facial mask once a week.

This year you feel like you're running
your life instead of your life running you.

⊚

They come up with new software
that makes your job immensely easier.

⊚

This year you nurture your creativity.

⊚

Depending on the state of your thighs,
you start or stop wearing stretch pants.

⊚

An older guy flirts with you.

⊚

A younger guy flirts with you.

You shiver with delight when you
wake up and remember it's your birthday.

◎

You accept yourself for who you really are,
not who you think you're supposed to be.

◎

You take the vacation of your
choice with the person of your choice.

◎

Today, instead of curling up in
a corner and crying about your birthday,
you go out and have a great time!

◎

You stop worrying about what's
on your Permanent Record.

At the next important meeting,
you crack a joke that breaks the tension,
makes everyone laugh, and gets the
discussion going in a positive direction.

You get out of the comfort zone—and love it.

You wipe out your outstanding debt.

Each guest at your birthday party
tells a flattering story about you.

Today your sweetheart whispers
sweet nothings in your ear.

This year you do whatever it is that you've
been promising yourself for years you'd do.
(And you know what it is!)

❂

At the end of a great birthday, you fall into
bed with your makeup still on. Just this once.

❂

Tonight you have beautiful dreams.